FINAL MYSTERY

The Truth About Death Revealed!

DOUG BATCHELOR

D0483588

Roseville, CA

Final Mystery:
The Truth About Death Revealed

By Doug Batchelor

Copyright © 2014 Amazing Facts

Printed in the USA
Published by Amazing Facts, Inc.
P.O. Box 1058
Roseville, CA 95678-8058
800-538-7275

Unless otherwise noted, Scripture taken
from the New King James Version®.
Copyright © 1982 by Thomas Nelson, Inc.
Used by permission. All rights reserved.

Scripture marked KJV is from
The Holy Bible, King James Version.

Cover Design by Haley Trimmer
Text Design by Greg Solie • Altamont Graphics

ISBN: 978-1-58019-622-2

Contents

Part One

Part Two

FINAL MYSTERY

The Truth About Death Revealed!

Part One

A Rude Revelation

Sitting with my grandfather in the living room and gazing at his black-and-white television, I watched as the costumed man, wearing what looked to be a small Mickey Mouse hat, danced around in a large dirt arena and teased a menacing bull.

After provoking the beast into a charge, the bullfighter would then stab a decorated dart into the back of the unlucky creature. This behavior was confusing enough for me, a four-year-old boy at the time, but then, as I looked on in wide-eyed horror, the angered bull successfully lunged and gored the matador, tossing him around the arena as if the man were not much more than a ragdoll. (Grandma would never have let me watch this if she were home!)

I sat there stunned, watching as attendants distracted the bull and others carried the limp body of the bullfighter from the ring. I asked my grandfather, "Poppy, what happened to the man?"

He glibly answered, "He's dead, Dougie."

"Are they going to take him to the doctor to get a shot?" I asked, thinking of the most serious medical treatment I could imagine. A shot from the doctor would surely fix anything.

"No," Grandpa responded. "He's not coming back. He's deader than a doornail." I wasn't even sure what a doornail was, but I got his meaning—the matador's life was permanently over. I asked several more questions, but Grandpa concluded, "Everybody dies sooner or later, Dougie."

That's the day when the awful reality of death first hit me. Someday, I would have my last birthday party.

It eventually happens to most everyone. Soon after our minds develop a sense of self awareness, typically between the ages of three and four, we are confronted by the truth of our mortality. It might come following a question about a pet goldfish that went belly up, or about all those square stones in that big grassy park, or about where that Happy Meal hamburger we're eating really came from. But whatever

6

the case, the thought that we'll someday cease living can temporarily traumatize a kid. It's a rude awakening.

But then, no one really wants to talk about death. Who wants to be morbid? We quickly cover up the dead and whisk them away. Most people don't have a will or estate plan, leaving a disastrous mess for strangers and family to untangle, perhaps subconsciously thinking that if they ignore it, the grim reaper will simply pass them by. Nevertheless, at some point in our quiet moments, we are confronted by the truth that we are all living on a relentless conveyor belt leading toward the grave.

Understandably, this unsettling fact has more than a few people searching for information. What about you? Are you curious about your mortality and what, if anything, happens when you die? Are you filled with uncertainty? Have you heard countless conflicting theories about death?

Since death is an unavoidable part of life, we shouldn't ignore it. Rather, let's courageously face it head on and seek to understand it as best we can. And really ... wouldn't it be foolish not to? Imagine this conversation:

"Hi, Sally! What's new?"

"Not much, Bob. Except I'm going on a trip."

"Really! How long will you be gone?"

"Forever."

"No kidding? Forever? Well, where are you going?"

"Not sure."

"Wait," Bob says incredulously. "You're going somewhere forever and ever and you're not sure where to? Well, when are you going to find out?"

Sally pauses a moment and says, "I just don't want to think about it right now."

I've heard of newlyweds heading off on a surprise honeymoon, in which the groom refuses to tell his bride where he is taking her. (How would you know what to pack?) My wife, Karen, would never tolerate it, but I can imagine someone being willing to not know where they're going in a case like that.

Yet who wouldn't want to know where they are going for forever ... *especially if they can know?*

This book is designed to address the truth about the great final mystery of life on earth:

death. What is on the other side of that enigmatic door?

The good news is you don't need to be afraid, so let's find out!

Where Do We Go For Answers?

Roughly 98 percent of the world's views regarding death falls within one of seven categories: Hinduism, Buddhism, Animism, Christianity, Islamism, Judaism, or atheism—including all of their various sects and factions.

These seven primary perspectives about death cover a wide spectrum, from a total cessation of existence to perfect consciousness and spiritual oneness with the divine.

For example, Hinduism teaches that souls are immortal and imperishable. Following death, a being might experience a period of rest before returning to earth to reincarnate and continue its "journey" toward ultimate oneness with divinity.

Similarly for Buddhists, death is not the end, but merely the end of the body we inhabit in this life. They believe their spirits live on and will seek attachment to a new body and a new life. What they are reborn as is the result of the past accumulation of positive and negative action in their lives, or karma.

Animism teaches that a dead person's spirit remains disembodied but is united with ancestors that, like ghosts, hang around the vicinity of their earthly lives. They also believe everything—including rivers, trees, rocks—has its own spirit.

Most atheists, of course, believe all life is the result of biological evolution, a series of remarkable but purely naturalistic processes that can be completely explained by science. Following death, all consciousness ceases as the body decomposes back into simple elements. That's all there is in life and death.

The three major monotheistic religions of Christianity, Judaism, and Islam all basically teach that we have one life on this planet to determine our eternal destiny. Following death, there will be a great judgment day, at which time individuals will be rewarded based on either their faith, good deeds, or both, resulting in some version of eternal paradise or lasting punishment. For instance, the Christian Bible says, "It is appointed for men to die once, but after this the judgment" (Hebrews 9:27).

There are, I suppose, many other possible scenarios that humans have yet considered or devised—but since we have only limited space, let's focus on the beliefs we already mentioned. As you can see for yourself, they are quite diverse and contradictory!

So where do we begin on a journey to understand the truth about death with so many options to consider? What will be our foundation of truth in understanding the ultimate mystery? Should we just put on a blindfold and play "pin the tail on the donkey"?

I don't think we should leave it up to chance, because I believe not understanding the truth on this subject can leave us wide open to major diabolical deceptions and could, in fact, affect our eternal destinies. That's why I need to be perfectly clear, upfront, about where I'm coming from and why.

Growing up, I believed like the atheists, that death was the absolute end of consciousness. But then I saw too many things happening to me and around me that led me to believe there must be some kind of divine power at work. Initially, I shifted in my thinking toward Eastern religions and believed in a form of reincarnation. But then, as a young adult, I moved up into the mountains and lived something like a hermit for a year-and-a-half.

That's when I discovered a Bible that someone had left behind, and I started reading it. From that time till today, nothing else makes as much sense to me or better explains the world in which we live. Because of my own personal journey and experience, as well as the evidence of science and a little common sense, this book approaches the great final mystery from the perspective of the Old and New Testament Scriptures.

That's my starting point. And what I've found in Scripture is often at odds with what I see in the mainstream. I assure you that what you're about to discover not only makes the most sense, but it will actually surprise and delight you.

So here we go …

Back From the Beyond?

"Clear!" The ER doctor's voice rings out like a thunderclap as the medical staff around her desperately races to save the life of the man teetering on the edge of death. As the heart monitor's beeping fades and then completely flat-lines, the doctor sends yet another wave of electricity through the limp body, which responds with contorts and twitches on the cold medical table—but nothing else happens … or does it?

Actually, someone has been watching this entire scene play out before him as he floats, disembodied, above the operating table. He soon recognizes that it is his own face and body lying lifeless below him, as a herd of doctors, nurses, and technicians continue to work feverishly around him.

But instead of feeling panic and fear, he feels total peace.

Soon, he begins to drift higher, ever higher, even through the hospital ceilings, as if being pulled by an unseen force into space. Along this supernatural journey, this spirit form finds himself in a grand, beautifully illuminated tunnel, floating toward the most stunning, comforting light he has ever seen.

Then, just as he reaches the end of the tunnel, a wave of warm light envelopes him and he steps into a glowing paradise. Immediately he recognizes faces he hasn't seen in years— old friends and even his parents—who aren't old anymore like he remembers them, but young and full of life.

Yet even better, he kneels down to embrace the child he lost to a sudden sickness so many years ago. Tears of joy and relief cascade down his cheeks as he hears his child's voice again. His parents and friends approach and receive him into their arms, washing him in their unconditional love and acceptance.

Until suddenly, out of nowhere, he feels himself pulled away from them. Now, in the blink of an eye, he is back on earth … the heart monitor detects a faint pulse, his lungs suddenly begin to breathe again, and his eyes flutter open. He's back on the hospital room table.

Groggy and confused, through the noise of the humming life-saving machines and the exclamations of relief from the ER staff, he wonders, "Was it all just some ethereal dream? It seemed so real!"

Near-Death Experiences

You've likely seen or heard some version of this scenario play out in countless movies, television shows, and even read books from authors who claimed to have had similar supernatural experiences.

A man, woman, or child dies—or at least seems to die—on the operating table or in an ambulance and has what is known as an "out-of-body experience," as if the consciousness, the mind's eye, indeed, the very soul, seems to have left the body and is freely roaming to other places on earth and even in heaven.

What is an out-of-body experience? "A vivid feeling of being detached from one's body, usually involving observing it and its environment from nearby."
—*Dictionary.com*

Nearly 20 percent of people who have been resuscitated after cardiac arrest have reported some form of near-death experience (NDE) or out-of-body experience (OBE).

Some have even said that during these events, they've come face-to-face with Jesus, Mary, John the Baptist, or any number of other famous Bible characters. Others say they've actually met a sister or brother or other family member who died long before they were even born, often providing details that would otherwise be unknown to them.

These messages certainly seem to convey hope, don't they? … that life really goes on after death. Who can deny the peace these experiences bring to the heart, to imagine that your grandmother, father, sister, or even your precious child is watching over you from heaven, where they are enjoying indescribable bliss?

Yet—if you think about this particular concept of heaven for too long, you might start to ask some, well, awkward questions:

- If grandma is in heaven watching over me, can she see *everything* I'm doing?

- Can heaven really be a place of joy for grandma if she's watching loved ones on earth experience terrible heartache, horrible sickness, and debilitating pain?

Does the Bible address difficult questions like these?

You might be surprised, but Scripture answers these questions in a frank and straightforward way. In fact, it actually offers a more realistic—and I'd venture an even more logical, scientific, and even peaceful—view of life after death.

But before I go any further, let me be perfectly clear: You can be absolutely reassured that there really is a heaven you can someday enjoy—but, yes, there is also that other destination too. For that, the Bible's teachings are very clear and convincing!

For instance, Jesus alluded to all this when He said, "Do not marvel at this; for the hour is coming in which all who are in the graves will hear His voice and come forth—those who have done good, to the resurrection of life, and those who have done evil, to the resurrection of condemnation" (John 5:28, 29).

In fact, what if Scripture offers an even better picture of the afterlife than the one you've heard from Hollywood or read in popular books? Wouldn't you like to know about it?

I believe that God's Word shares something utterly unique about the reality of the physical and spiritual—the body and the soul—than what you've likely been taught all your life, and that the truth will not only make sense and bring you peace and assurance, it will set you free from very real dangers (John 8:32).

A little later in this book, we'll be discovering the amazing glories of heaven. You might even be tempted to jump to that part now, but before we can get to heaven, so to speak, we need to study and understand the subject of death. So hang in there, it will be worth it!

So what about those who report near-death experiences?

As the name implies, an NDE is when a person comes close to dying or, in some cases, is clinically dead for a few brief moments. While similar to out-of-body experiences, these are somewhat different in that they only occur when, of course, a person is near death. (An out-of-body experience can result at any time, perhaps as a result of brief oxygen depravation or while under the influence of drugs, for instance.)

The question we need to answer is whether the visions that some people report as an NDE are true. If they aren't really seeing Jesus or their loved ones in heaven, who or what could they be seeing? The most important thing I want you to remember here is that we should never build our understanding of Scripture based on an individual's personal experience, including mine! Always base it on the Word of God.

But first, I believe there is a scientific/medical explanation we should consider. A doctor recently explained to me that what often happens during extreme heart trauma is the brain is deprived of oxygen. Obviously, it's very dangerous when you don't get enough oxygen. As a scuba diver, I know what can happen when the brain is deprived of even the right mixture of oxygen. We call it "raptures of the deep." You can hallucinate and have all kinds of strange visions. It's actually a predictable biological occurrence. So a person who claims to have risen out of their body during a near-death moment might have simply experienced a physiological phenomenon resulting from a lack of oxygen.

The well-known Hungarian neurologist Dr. Ladislas J. Meduna (1896–1964) conducted a number of experiments during which he administered to patients a mixture of air made of 30 percent carbon dioxide and 70 percent oxygen. By doing so, he was able to consistently reproduce among his subjects the sensation of an OBE. One subject said, "I felt as though I was looking down at myself, as though I was way out here in space. ... I felt sort of separated."

This could be true of anyone who experiences any kind of brain trauma or a medical condition that causes a lack of oxygen to the brain, whether through an injury or even in taking powerful prescription drugs. These experiences can seem so real and vivid that the sights and sounds and smells during these "visions" seem tangible to those who have experienced them.

Dr. Bruce Greyson, a psychiatrist at the University of Virginia, is one of the foremost experts of near-death experiences, having studied more than 100 incidents of near-death patients. From his work, he has learned that several patients have recounted experiencing a sense of peace, love, and a stark feeling of "leaving the physical." Sometimes they claimed to have encountered deities or deceased loved ones. Interestingly, did you know that those who experience this phenomenon in non-Christian countries have claimed to have encountered Mohammed, Krishna, and Buddha?

Likewise Dr. Wendy Wright, a neurologist from Emory University, believes that near-death experiences are a direct result of endorphin release in the brain. "When these chemicals are released, these different types of phenomena can occur: a person might see a light, or experience a sense of peace or calming [and] feel that they're surrounded by loved ones." Such visions, although comforting, are little more than "tricks of the brain," she says.

Of course, I want to be very careful not to totally rule out the possibility that God is trying to speak to an individual personally through a dream or vision. Yes, God can even communicate some personal message to an individual through one of these near-death events. The Bible tells us about many instances in which God used dreams and visions to communicate to His people. But as I mentioned and must mention again, we need to be very careful to never build our theology on these individual dreams or near-death experiences, because they're all a little different and they often contradict each other.

What Is Life?

Throughout history, we find people from all walks of life who claim they've had these out-of-body experiences, enabling their ethereal souls to leave their physical bodies and witness other planes of existence.

> What is a near-death experience? "A sensation or vision, as of the afterlife, reported by a person who has come close to death." —*Dictionary.com*

Those who have these experiences often report having died first, if briefly—but not always, as in the case of the NDE reported in the popular book and film *Heaven Is for Real*. However it happens, they say their immortal souls left their bodies and were caught up into heaven, where they interacted with angels, loved ones, and other heavenly beings.

Conversely, in 2009, a woman named Tamara Laroux says after she successfully committed suicide, her soul left her body and actually plummeted straight into hell, where she experienced enormous suffering before the "vessel of God laid her soul back in her body" and restored her to life.

That's an amazing, mysterious picture. But is it real? Is it biblical?

While it's certainly true that we still don't understand all the mysteries of life and death, the Bible has some very eye-opening things to say about the nature of life, death, the body, and the soul. You might be surprised to learn that what the Bible says is perhaps the total opposite of what you've heard from a preacher on TV or even in your church's pulpit.

But will you agree with me that it is only God's Word that will help us pierce through all the fog of human emotion that can cloud and confuse our understanding? The Bible alone can bring sound answers and satisfying assurance for those who fear the future and who wonder what happens to the soul a few short moments after death.

So according to the Bible, what is life? Ironically, to first understand the nature of death, we have to begin with life. And for the answer, we will need to go back to the beginning.

1. Genesis 2:7 says, "The LORD God formed man of the dust of the ground."

Here Scripture tells us that Adam's body was designed by God and contained all the elements necessary for life … yet there was no life. The heart wasn't beating. The lungs weren't breathing. The brain wasn't thinking. He was formed but still lifeless.

Instead, God did one more thing …

2. The Lord "breathed into his nostrils the breath of life; and man *became* a living soul" (Genesis 2:7 KJV).

Now, I have emphasized the word "became" in this passage because people often miss it. They miss that God did not *put* a soul into the body at the creation. Instead, He added something called the "breath." As a result of the body and breath uniting, man *became* a soul.

What is a soul? According to the Bible, the "body" plus "breath of life" makes a living soul.

What Is This "Breath of Life"?

What then is this thing the Bible calls the "breath"?

The Scripture says, "For as the body without the *spirit* is dead, so faith without works is dead also" (James 2:26). I have highlighted the word "spirit" in this passage because it's very significant. Check your Bible's references or, perhaps, a concordance, and you'll see that the word for "spirit" is also the same word used for "breath."

That word being translated as "breath" is from the root word in the Greek, "pneuma," a word that means "breath" or "air."

> The English word "pneumonia" is derived from *pneuma*, because it is a disease of the lungs, or of breathing. Or when a mechanic uses "pneumatic" tools, he is using tools that are operated by air.

Now, that same Greek word "pneuma" also means "spirit." For example, the Greek term for "Holy Spirit" is "hagios pneumatos," meaning "Holy Breath" or "Holy Spirit."

Why does this matter? Well, the words "breath" and "spirit" are often used interchangeably in the Bible. For example, Job said, "All the while my *breath* is in me, and the *spirit* of God is in my nostrils" (Job 27:3). Do you see the two words I've italicized—"breath" and "spirit"? Job was describing the very same thing by those words; in fact, in original language, they are the very same words. He's saying that man has this breath of life in his nostrils and that is what God breathed into man's nostrils at the time of creation.

Remember, "The LORD God formed man of the dust of the ground, and breathed into his nostrils the breath of life; and man became a living soul" (Genesis 2:7 KJV). God didn't breathe a bodiless soul into Adam ... He breathed life into Adam! Then Adam himself *became* a soul.

Mortal Being vs. Immortal Soul?

The Bible says, "Shall mortal man be more just than God?" (Job 4:17 KJV). Job was a man beloved by God, a man who knew the Word of God and strived to live a righteous life. And according to Job and the Bible, man is mortal.

> What does "mortal" mean? It means "subject to death." What does immortal mean? It means "not subject to death." —*Dictionary.com*

We know this because God told Adam and Eve in the beginning that if they disobeyed His commands, they would die (Genesis 2:17). It meant that man has always been subject to death. He is not, by nature, an immortal creature.

In fact, the only time the word "immortal" is ever used in the Bible, it is referring to God: "Now unto the King eternal, immortal, invisible, the only wise God, be honor and glory for ever and ever. Amen" (1 Timothy 1:17 KJV).

God is the author of life, the source of all existence. From Him all life in the universe comes: "The King of kings and Lord of lords, *who alone has immortality*, dwelling in unapproachable light, whom no man has seen or can see, to whom be honor and everlasting power" (1 Timothy 6:15, 16, my emphasis).

In case you missed it, the Bible says that God alone is immortal—the only being in the universe that has always lived and isn't subject to death. God is infinite, but angels and humans are finite. We were created, and if we were created, it also means we can be "uncreated" or destroyed. If we can be destroyed, we cannot be immortal. At least not yet...

But wait. Is it possible, however, that while we have a mortal body, we have an immortal soul attached to us? Perhaps the "real" person is not the body at all, but the undying soul dwelling within the mortal body. You might be thinking, "Doesn't the Bible say that when we die, the spirit returns to God?"

Yes, and these are excellent questions often asked by those who have been taught that humans are immortal by nature. They are critical questions that have, in fact, very clear Bible answers. Let's take a few moments to get to the bottom of it.

What Is Death?

Suppose someone is sentenced to death for murder, but just a moment or two after they are executed, they suddenly regain consciousness and are put in prison again. That doesn't sound like "death" was much of a sentence, does it?

Yet this is how we treat the Bible, which spends a great deal of time telling us that death is a terrible thing foisted on mankind because of sin. It tells us death isn't really our natural state; we all strive to stay alive, kicking and fighting against death at all costs. We were meant for eternity from the beginning, and sin and death are an unnatural interruption of God's plan for a happy and abundant life.

> Death is "a permanent cessation of all vital functions: the end of life." —*Merriam Webster*

And yet many believe that death hardly interrupts anything at all, because they believe the moment we die, for all intents and purposes, we immediately bounce back to life again.

So going back to our previous section, what sense does it make for the Bible to tell us we are mortal only to really mean that we're immortal? When the Bible says that God alone is immortal and that man is mortal, why do we not believe it?

This is the common perception even in the Christian world. The moment we die, our conscious spirit goes straight to heaven. After all, the Bible says, "Then the dust will return to the earth as it was, and the spirit will return to God who gave it" (Ecclesiastes 12:7).

After death the Bible says everything goes back from where it came. The body returns to the earth as dust, and the spirit, or breath of life, returns to God.

Death, it seems, is just the opposite of creation. Of course, we all know about the process of body decomposition. When the body dies, the cells immediately begin to decompose and break down into their basic chemical elements, which get absorbed into the ground.

And this makes perfect sense when we read about the spirit returning to the God who gave it. When the Bible described the "spirit" returning to God, it has to be referring to the breath of life, because that was what God gave in the beginning. Because death is the opposite of creation, the only thing that could now "return" to the One who gave it is the breath of life, which God gave to man when he was created.

Many Bibles with marginal notes or a concordance refer to the breath of life in Genesis 7:22 as "the breath of the spirit of life."

Psalm 104:29, 30, says, "You take away their breath, they die and return to their dust. You send forth Your Spirit, they are created." This passage reveals that we're right on track with our understanding of the spirit according to the Bible. It reverses the order of creation, using the same word for "breath," even though some translations issue this word as "spirit." There is simply no reason to do this. It only makes sense when we understand that the two words "breath" and "spirit" are used interchangeably and mean the same thing.

To be clear, the "spirit of life" is not necessarily the same as the Holy Spirit; neither is the "breath of life" the same as the regular air we breathe. This breath or spirit is the special, life-giving power of God that makes the body a functioning organism. Nothing more, and nothing less—which isn't to say it's not miraculous, because it is!

Still, in the Bible, except perhaps in poetical or allegorical usage, the soul does not go in and out of the body; neither does it have an independent existence outside of the body. Because the Greek word "psuche," meaning "life," has sometimes been translated as "soul" in the King James Version, some have drawn wrong, often superficial conclusions that the soul is a ghost; but only because they apply an incorrect definition to the word "soul."

Many Christians have been taught that the "soul" possesses a natural immortality, and every time they read or hear the word "soul," they assume that it's referring to the immortal part of a human they've always been told about. But as we've already learned, not even one time in the Bible is the "soul" referred to as being immortal or undying. That designation belongs only to the Creator.

The plain truth is that the "soul" is the conscious life that resulted when God added the breath—or spirit—to the body. A simple illustration helps makes this easy to understand:

> Let's say that the electric current that flows into a light bulb represents the breath of life, which God put into the body, and the light itself represents the soul, which man became after the breath joined the body. That shining light is a near perfect representation of

the completed creation. But now let's flip the switch, disconnecting the electric power, and turn the light off. What happened? The light "died." The current leaves the bulb, just as the breath leaves the body at death. Now where is the light? Did it go up into the electric socket? No, it simply ceased to exist when the current separated from the bulb. So where is the soul when the breath separates from the body? There is no soul—because it ceases to be until, of course, God restores the breath of life to the new body in the resurrection.

This should put to rest the idea that before creation, man existed in a disembodied form. Indeed, there was no personality, no conscious emotion, before God added the breath to the body. Only at that moment did man "became a living soul." If the soul came to be as a result of the union between body and breath, when does the soul cease to be? When the breaking of that union occurs.

Remember, according to the Bible, the "body" plus "breath" makes a living soul. The Lord "breathed into his nostrils the breath of life; and man became a living soul" (Genesis 2:7).

Now here's a surprise: Even animals are referred to as "souls" in the Bible—in the exact same way humans are referred to as souls. Why? Because they have the same breath from God to make them live. The King James says, "Every living soul died in the sea" (Revelation 16:3 KJV).

The Bible teaches, "What happens to the sons of men also happens to animals; one thing befalls them: as one dies, so dies the other. Surely, they all have one breath; man has no advantage over animals, for all is vanity. All go to one place: all are from the dust, and all return to dust." (Ecclesiastes 3:19, 20).

This does not mean that man and animals have the same ultimate end. Humans have been made in God's image and will be redeemed by Christ. However, the important point is that the life of all creatures comes only from God, whether it be human or animal. And that life, the one you now experience with your body, is often referred to in many Bible translations as the "soul."

What Did Jesus Say?

Interestingly, in the book of Job, the writer, whom many scholars believe to be Moses, describes a period of unconscious sleep in the grave before awaking to receive his eternal reward. This also happens to agree with the prophet Daniel, who spoke of the coming of Christ in these words: "And many of those who sleep in the dust of the earth shall awake, some to everlasting life, some to shame and everlasting contempt" (Daniel 12:2).

That brings up an interesting question: Why do so many Bible writers speak of death as a sleep? I believe because it is a perfect analogy of the true state of the dead. When a tired person lies down at night, they are wrapped in blissful sleep. As far as they are concerned, the very next moment they are awakened by the rising sun. They are totally unconscious of anything that transpired while they slept.

So it can be said that death is really just a brief unconscious "sleep."

We can trust what Jesus said, right? Well, this is exactly how He described it.

When Lazarus died, Jesus said to His disciples, " 'Our friend Lazarus sleeps, but I go that I may wake him up.' Then His disciples said, 'Lord, if he sleeps he will get well.' However, Jesus spoke of his death, but they thought that He was speaking about taking rest in sleep. Then Jesus said to them plainly, 'Lazarus is dead' " (John 11:11–14).

Christ clearly called death a sleep. Later, He stood by the tomb of His friend and cried out, "Lazarus, come forth!" Notice, He did not say, "Lazarus, come down." Lazarus was not up in heaven. Nor did Jesus say "Lazarus, come up," because his friend was not down in hades burning—nor was Lazarus anywhere else, except inside the walls of his tomb. In response to the call of Jesus, Lazarus awoke from his sleep of death and walked out into the sunlight.

This is one of the most incredible miracles of Jesus, because Lazarus had been dead for four days. His sisters even protested when Jesus ordered the stone to be rolled away from the tomb door. Martha said, "Lord, by this time there is a stench" (John 11:39), because the decomposition of Lazarus' body had certainly already begun. Yet Jesus insisted that Lazarus had been asleep.

Let's look at it this way—what if there was an immortal soul and Lazarus had gone to heaven? Would Lazarus really have wanted to come back to this sin-filled world after being in the holy presence of God? Had he truly been enjoying the rewards of the righteous for three days, would he have sought or agreed to return to a world full of pain, misery, aging, and death?

If Lazarus had been going through an out-of-body experience for four days, it is a bit strange for the Bible writers to leave that information out. It doesn't prove or disprove anything here, but the Bible's silence regarding Lazarus' heavenly experience is certainly puzzling. And not just silence about his experience, but the experiences of the dozens of people who the Bible tells us were resurrected. I think that speaks volumes, don't you?

Jesus used simple terminology in describing death as a sleep, and we have no problem understanding the nature of sleep.

Let's say a man falls asleep on his couch, but he has a heart attack in the middle of the night and passes away. According to the popular view of death, this man who knew nothing while he was sleeping suddenly knows everything as his soul leaves his body. But how could that be true? Jesus said death is a sleep. If the man knew nothing while sleeping, how could he know any more after his death? Christ's words would have no meaning if we twist them to say that death isn't really like a dreamless sleep, but just an immediate passageway to a different conscious life.

Thankfully, we are not left to wonder about the true nature of death. Many Bible writers give even more detailed explanations of what it is like. "Do not put your trust in princes, nor in a son of man, in whom there is no help. His spirit departs, he returns to his earth; in that very day his plans perish" (Psalm 146:3, 4).

The writers of the Bible most often talked about the unconscious nature of death. They never spoke of the exciting descriptions of life after death that we might expect if people went to heaven after they died. King David said, "His spirit departs, he returns to his earth; in that very day his thoughts perish" (Psalm 146:4). His son Solomon, considered the wisest man who ever lived, added;

> For the living know that they will die; but the dead know nothing, and they have no more reward, for the memory of them is forgotten. Also their love, their hatred, and their envy have now perished; nevermore will they have a share in anything done under the sun. ... There is no work or device or knowledge or wisdom in the grave where you are going (Ecclesiastes 9:5, 6, 10).

Should we take this to mean that because there is "no work or device" when we die, we won't be doing anything at all in heaven? What else could Solomon have meant if he didn't believe that death is simply an unconscious sleep? He would have known that an immortal soul would go on to do something—that our wisdom and thoughts would not perish. Instead of describing death as a dreamless sleep, he would have said, "Their love, and their hatred, and their envy will continue ... for there is work and knowledge and wisdom where you are going." Such an unambiguous statement would have certainly cleared it up.

But the Bible has no such statement; instead, it repeatedly says the opposite. We read, "For [the grave] cannot thank You, death cannot praise You; those who go down to the pit cannot hope for Your truth. The living, the living man, he shall praise You, as I do this day" (Isaiah 38:18, 19). Would not the saved who have died be praising God if they were ushered into heaven right after their death? The Bible repeats the same idea: "The dead do not praise the LORD, nor any who go down into silence" (Psalm 115:17). "For in death there is no remembrance of You; in the grave who will give You thanks?" (Psalm 6:5).

Can Souls Die?

It's not surprising that those who say they went to heaven or hell after death and returned believe that humans do have a soul that is separate and distinct from their physical bodies.

This same idea allows people to believe that even if they haven't died, their souls can still go to heaven or separate from their bodies through "astral projection." (This is not meant to say a person cannot be taken off in vision and shown things by God, as with the apostle John in the book of Revelation.)

But the Bible makes a staggering statement that denies this premise. Even if there was a distinct soul separate from the body, the Bible still says, "Behold, all souls are Mine; ... the soul who sins shall die" (Ezekiel 18:4). If the soul can experience death, then by definition, it cannot be immortal. This assures us that no part of a human being could be classified as immortal.

Even Jesus weighed in on this very idea when, in Matthew 10:28, He says, "Do not fear those who kill the body but cannot kill the soul. But rather fear Him who is able to destroy both soul and body in hell." The Bible teaches that the soul can die in the fires of hell. Therefore, it cannot be immortal by nature.

This information can be shocking to hear. Most of us have been told exactly opposite of this. But it's absolutely true—in all 1,700 occurrences of the words "soul" and "spirit" in the Bible, not once do they refer to a being who is immortal or undying.

The Immortal Soul

Where, then, did the belief that we have immortal souls come from? You've probably heard about the "soul that never dies" from your earliest years of childhood. One thing is certain: As we learned from the Bible, it did not originate in Scripture.

The truth is that it came directly from pagan traditions and mythologies. For instance, ancient Chinese ancestor-worship was rooted in the belief that the soul did not die. Egyptian pyramid hieroglyphics reveal that a doctrine of immortality was basic to their worship of the sun god. In India, the Hindus believe strongly in reincarnation and transmigration of the soul.

There is a compelling clue in the Bible that tells us how the belief got started in the first place ...

Now the serpent was more cunning than any beast of the field which the LORD God had made. And he said to the woman, "Has God indeed said, 'You shall not eat of every tree of the garden'?" And the woman said to the serpent, "We may eat the fruit of the trees of the garden; but of the fruit of the tree which is in the midst of the garden, God has said, 'You shall not eat it, nor shall you touch it, lest you die'" (Genesis 3:1–4).

Somebody disagreed with God. The Creator had declared that sin would bring death, but Satan said the exact opposite, "You will not really die."

That was the first recorded lie on earth, and the one who told it has been trying to uphold it ever since. This first deception on human immortality has been repeated many times through the years, often by preachers and theologians who simply don't know any better. Perhaps unwittingly, they end up making the same claims that the devil makes—that there isn't really any death no matter what you do.

Can this teaching actually be dangerous? Indeed, it involves much more than merely advancing a false statement. The implications are far-reaching. Millions will be deceived because they do not understand the truth about the state of man in death. Deception on this point opens a door that can flood our minds with darkness and open us up to demonic suggestion—more on this vital point later. The only protection we will ever have against this insidious danger is to know the truth about death and the soul. "Our Savior Christ Jesus, who abolished death and brought life and immortality to light through the gospel …" (2 Timothy 1:11).

Do the Dead Talk to the Living?

In her book *Like Lambs to the Slaughter*, Johanna Michaelson tells of a seven-year-old girl who was visited one night by an angelic being. The beautiful apparition was radiant, aglow with a warm soft light. "I am an angel sent from Jesus," the being told the girl. The child was from a deeply committed Christian family, and she loved Jesus. Nevertheless, she was incredibly frightened by the presence of the "angel."

"You're not from Jesus," the little girl retorted.

"How do you know?" the shining angel replied.

"Because in the Bible every real angel said, 'Be not afraid' if someone was afraid of him. I'm afraid now, and you didn't say that to me."

Immediately the glowing being transformed into a hideous demon and swooped down threateningly upon her. "Would you rather see me like this?" it shrieked, and then it vanished into the dark.

If Satan or one of his demons appeared to you as an angel from heaven, would you be able to unmask the imposter? Would you be as discerning as this little girl? Or would its heavenly disguise and message trick you?

Why do so many disbelieve what the Bible clearly says about death? Of course, many are raised to believe differently, and it's just habit. Others simply don't know what their Bibles actually say.

But there is also much more involved. Many sincerely believe that they have eye-witness proof that the dead do in fact return. They either know someone or believe they have personally witnessed it with their own senses, seeing or even conversing with departed loved ones.

What can be said about these manifestations? People can give the place, date, and hour when they were confronted by dead relatives or friends in exactly the same form as when they lived. Sometimes this happened here on earth; at other times, these people had a dream and believe they went to heaven to see their loved ones there.

Do we discount all such appearances as mental aberrations of emotional, unstable individuals? I don't believe we can.

Yet while it might be true that ethereal forms can appear to genuine people, on the basis of God's Word, we simply cannot accept that these manifestations are real spirits of the dead. We know what the Bible says—the dead cannot return; neither do they have an existence in any conscious, living form whatsoever.

So the question becomes, who is masquerading in these bodily forms and making bold claims in the name and likeness of the dead?

Who else, indeed, but the devil, the father of lies, who built his first deception around the issue of death? He disguised himself as a serpent and contradicted God when he said to Eve, "You shall not surely die." When death did follow, Satan tried to make the living believe it was only an illusion. By impersonating those who died, he has persuaded millions that he was right and God was wrong. Accepting the testimony of their eyes and ears above the testimony of the Bible, many have become so-called experts in calling up the spirits in séances. You can find a program featuring these spiritualists on some channel at just about any time of day.

And don't you see? It's the perfect setup for Satan to exploit the grief of those who have lost relatives, attempting to draw them into his spiritualistic snare by pretending to be a special loved one. It can be an overwhelming delusion! Only those who have known the truth can withstand this type of attack.

The Witch of Endor

John Bowman was a wealthy tanner who made his fortune by selling leather goods to the North during the Civil War.

Yet while his business life was successful, Bowman's domestic life was tragic. His first daughter, Addie, died in 1854 at only four months old. A second daughter, Ella, grew to a young adult but died in 1879. The final blow came a few months later when his wife, Jennie, perished. Grief-stricken and pining for his family, Bowman built an elaborate memorial for them in a Cuttingsville, Vermont, cemetery.

The grand mausoleum was comprised of 750 tons of granite and 50 tons of marble. It cost $75,000 to build, a fortune in the 1800s.

The interior of the tomb featured sculptures of the deceased and ornate stonework around the crypts. Mirrors were positioned inside to make the room seem even larger. Bowman also had a famous sculptor create a life-sized marble figure of himself kneeling with a key in hand, installing it outside on the tomb's steps. The statue symbolized his desire to unlock the graves of his family.

When completed in 1881, the mausoleum became something of a tourist attraction. Thousands converged on the cemetery to gawk. Bowman had a guestbook placed inside the chamber and even hired an usher to conduct short tours. But he still wanted to be closer to his deceased family, so he built an elaborate home for himself right across the street from the tomb.

Evidently, John came to believe his family would join him in the house after his death, so before he died, he created a trust fund that would provide for the complete maintenance of his house. For 50 years, till the last of the funds ran out, the house furniture was dusted every day, the beds changed every week, and fresh food put in the pantry, ostensibly waiting for Bowman and his family to return. Yet year after year, the house stood vacant and, evidently, the owners never returned.

Of course, this is consistent with what the Bible has always taught, that the dead do not return to their homes or communicate with the living. "As the cloud disappears and vanishes away, so he who goes down to the grave does not come up. He shall never return to his house, nor shall his place know him anymore" (Job 7:9, 10). Had Bowman known the truth, maybe he could have used that money in better ways.

But did you know there was a famous Bible character—a king of Israel, no less—who also rejected God's Word on the state of the dead? He chose to believe that the living can communicate with the dead. And like Bowman, it did not end well for him.

His name was Saul, and we find this piece of his story in 1 Samuel 28:11–15, where the aged king tries to communicate with the dead prophet through the medium of a witch.

> Then the woman said, "Whom shall I bring up for you?" And he said, "Bring Samuel up for me." When the woman saw Samuel, she cried out with a loud voice. And the woman spoke to Saul, saying, "Why have you deceived me? For you are Saul!" And the king said to her, "Do not be afraid. What did you see? " And the woman said to Saul, "I

saw a spirit ascending out of the earth."
So he said to her, "What is his form?"
And she said, "An old man is coming
up, and he is covered with a mantle."
And Saul perceived that it was Samuel,
and he stooped with his face to the
ground and bowed down. Now Samuel
said to Saul, "Why have you disturbed
me by bringing me up?" And Saul answered, "I am deeply distressed; for the
Philistines make war against me, and
God has departed from me and does
not answer me anymore, neither by
prophets nor by dreams. Therefore I
have called you, that you may reveal to
me what I should do."

The story of the witch of Endor tells a sad
tale of the destructive results of disobedience
toward God. Saul was once a powerful leader,
chosen by God to be the first king over Israel.
Initially, he was a mighty ruler and was filled
with the Spirit of God.

However, after a series of victorious bat-
tles, he became proud and jealous, more concerned with the adoration of the people than
the approval of God. Gradually, he hardened
his heart and rebelled against the command-
ments of God.

By the time he consulted the witch at Endor, he had become a desperate man.

His Philistine enemies had gathered a massive army to battle against the Israelites. The threat of this siege overwhelmed Saul with fear. God no longer answered his prayers, and he felt increasingly powerless against his enemies. In desperation, he located a witch and asked her to call up the spirit of the dead prophet Samuel, who had been his counselor while he was alive.

Many people use the story of Saul's encounter with this spirit as proof that people continue to live on in spiritual form after death. How else, they reason, can Samuel have appeared to Saul during this Old Testament séance?

I believe that some apparition did indeed appear to the witch of Endor, but it was not the spirit of Samuel the prophet. The Bible is very clear that demons can impersonate other beings, even ministers. "Satan himself transforms himself into an angel of light" (2 Corinthians 11:14).

Samuel was a faithful man for his entire life. He was dedicated to the service of God at his birth, and he received direct communications from heaven until his death. Unquestionably, he had God's favor. If he were alive in spiritual form after death, he would surely be in heaven in the presence of the Lord.

This should help us know the true nature of this spirit summoned by the witch. God had chosen to stop communicating with King Saul because of his rebellion and refusal to repent. First Samuel 28:6 makes God's silence plain: "When Saul inquired of the LORD, the LORD did not answer him, either by dreams or by Urim or by the prophets."

The Bible plainly states that God refused to speak to Saul through His prophets. Therefore, if Samuel were still alive, he would not have received any word from God to give to Saul. Yet the story tells us that the spirit "Samuel" did speak to Saul and even delivered a prophetic message to him (1 Samuel 28:16–19). If God did not speak to Saul through the prophets, yet Samuel delivered a prophetic message anyway, then Samuel would have been in rebellion against God. Why would Samuel, a man who was obedient to God every moment of his life, choose to rebel after his death? It's simply illogical.

And again, remember that God gave specific instructions to His people against performing witchcraft, sorcery, necromancy,

49

or even associating with people who did these things. The Bible plainly warns in Deuteronomy 18:10–12:

> There shall not be found among you anyone who makes his son or daughter pass through the fire, or one who practices witchcraft, or a soothsayer, or one who interprets omens, or a sorcerer, or one who conjures spells, or a medium, or a spiritist, or one who calls up the dead. For all who do these things are an abomination to the LORD.

Saul was well aware of this warning, too, because he had evicted all mediums from the land of Israel during his reign (1 Samuel 28:3). Therefore, when he consulted the witch at Endor, he was breaking God's command and his own command! Therefore, the spirit that appeared to him could not have been from heaven.

You will also notice that in verse 14, Saul asks, "What is his form?" He's asking the witch to tell him what the spirit looks like. So Saul isn't actually seeing anything—he's trusting the witch to tell him what she sees. And the message that the spirit gives is an utterly hopeless message—"You're going to die. Your sons are going to die." It really seems like the devil here is kicking Saul for the last time while he is down.

"Saul died for his unfaithfulness which he had committed against the LORD, because he did not keep the word of the LORD, and also because he consulted a medium for guidance" (1 Chronicles 10:13).

If the spirit wasn't Samuel, it could only have been a demon. Demons appearing to people on earth do not tell us anything about life after death.

Is this story an exceptional case? Unfortunately, no. Experiences like this have been repeated over and over again throughout history. Doubtless there are some people who create their own illusions, but we have to recognize that, very often, the devil is manipulating the minds of people by his supernatural expertise in deceit.

Think of the implications: Millions of people have literally submitted their lives to the control of demons, believing that they were being advised by loving relatives. Can you see the irony? Can you see how easily Satan can start controlling the lives of Christians who do not understand the true Bible teaching about death?

The only safety for anyone is the Word of God. Yet the stage is set for the majority of

Christians and other religious people to be swept away by the final manifestation of satanic power—all because they have been taught a lie about the state of man in death.

The Dying Thief and Jesus

People who believe the dead go directly to heaven or hell at death often bring up the conversation Jesus had with the thief on the cross.

In the last moments of his life, one of the thieves crucified beside Jesus calls out to Him. " 'Lord, remember me when You come into Your kingdom.' And Jesus said to him, 'Assuredly, I say to you, today you will be with Me in Paradise' " (Luke 23:42, 43).

At a superficial glance, it seems that Jesus was telling the dying criminal that he would go immediately to heaven on the very same day he died. But a careful study will help us harmonize this seeming contradiction.

Three days after Jesus spoke to the repentant thief, on the resurrection morning, He met Mary near the open tomb. As she fell at His feet to worship Him, Jesus said, "Do not cling to Me, for I have not yet ascended to My Father; but go to My brethren and say to them, 'I am ascending to My Father and

your Father, and to My God and your God'"
(John 20:17).

If Jesus had not yet gone to heaven by
Sunday morning, how could He have assured
the thief three days earlier that they would go
there together that same day? Obviously, if
Jesus had not gone to His Father by the time of
His resurrection, He could not have been with
the thief in paradise three days earlier.

We also need to be aware that the original manuscripts of the Bible were written
with no punctuation. In 1611 when the King
James Version was created, scholars separated
the words, inserted punctuation marks, and
divided the script into verses and chapters.
Although they generally did a tremendous
work, these men were not necessarily inspired.
So in Luke 23:43, they added a comma before the word "today," which makes Jesus say,
"Assuredly, I say to you, today you will be with
Me in Paradise."

But what if they had placed the comma after the word "today" instead of before it? Then
the sentence would read, "Assuredly, I say to
you today, you will be with Me in Paradise."
In other words, Jesus would be saying to the
thief, "I give you the assurance today—when
it seems that I can save no one, when my own
disciples have forsaken me and I am dying as

a condemned felon—I give you the assurance that you will be with me in paradise."

With all we've learned from the Bible, which makes more sense to you? Either we have to completely ignore Job, King Solomon, King David, and God Himself to accommodate the teaching of the immortal soul. Or to make this passage work, all we need to do is move the comma, which was placed hundreds of years later by translators who had a bias. Placing the comma after the word "today" is just as true to the original text as placing it before the word. The only difference is that one way brings total harmony in the Scriptures and the other brings a hopeless contradiction and confusion.

Also, keep in mind that the thief was only asking to be remembered when Jesus came into His kingdom. He did not request any reward on that day of his approaching death. In the same vein, we find the apostle Paul anticipating his departing this life, "For I am already being poured out as a drink offering, and the time of my departure is at hand. I have fought the good fight, I have finished the race, I have kept the faith. Finally, there is laid up for me the crown of righteousness, which the Lord, the righteous Judge, will give to me on that Day, and not to me only but also to all who have loved His appearing." (2 Timothy 4:6–8).

Just as the thief and Paul both focused their hope of eternal reward upon the coming of Christ's kingdom, so may we also be remembered in that day.

The Heaven Resurrection Sequence

In Peter's sermon on the day of Pentecost, he made this staggering revelation about King David, who had been dead for more than a thousand years: "David did not ascend into the heavens" (Acts 2:34). Though sometimes a wayward king, David had received the assurance of forgiveness and salvation. Why, then, was he not enjoying the bliss of heaven long centuries after his passing? The question is answered in verse 29, where Peter explains, "Men and brethren, let me speak freely to you of the patriarch David, that he is both dead and buried, and his tomb is with us to this day." What could be more to the point?

How interesting! If the man after God's own heart had not received his reward by a thousand years after his death, what about all the other saved people who had lived and died up to that time? According to the Bible, they, too, were resting in their graves, awaiting the resurrection.

Jesus said, "You will be blessed, because they cannot repay you; for you shall be repaid at the resurrection of the just" (Luke 14:14). Again, He said, "For the Son of Man will come in the glory of His Father with His angels, and then He will reward each according to his works" (Matthew 16:27). In simple, direct language, Jesus taught that no one would be rewarded until the resurrection takes place at His second coming. This means that none of the saved who have died have gone to heaven yet. All are still waiting—"sleeping"—in their graves for the judgment and the end of the world.

Some of the last few words of the Bible confirm this: "Behold, I am coming quickly, and My reward is with Me, to give to every one according to his work" (Revelation 22:12). This last-day reward is further described by the apostle Paul in 1 Corinthians 15:22, 23: "For as in Adam all die, even so in Christ all shall be made alive. But each one in his own order: Christ the firstfruits, afterward those who are Christ's at His coming." And again in verse 53, "This mortal must put on immortality." When does it happen? "In a moment, in the twinkling of an eye, at the last trumpet" (v. 52).

Now that we understand the fate of those saved in Christ, what do we know will happen to those who refuse the grace of Jesus? When will they be punished for their sins? The answer is found in 2 Peter 2:9, "The Lord knows how to deliver the godly out of temptations and to reserve the unjust under punishment for the day of judgment."

Do you see it? The wicked are *reserved* somewhere until the day of judgment arrives. Where are they reserved? Jesus answers the question in a verse we mentioned earlier, "Do not marvel at this; for the hour is coming in which all who are in the graves will hear His voice and come forth—those who have done good, to the resurrection of life, and those who have done evil, to the resurrection of condemnation" (John 5:28, 29).

The Savior made it exceedingly plain that everyone—the saved and the lost—would be reserved in their graves until the resurrection to life or the resurrection to condemnation. And it really makes a lot of sense to understand it in this way. Obviously, no one can be punished until after they are judged. Suppose someone came before the judge charged with stealing, and the judge said, "Put him away for nine years and then we will hear his case." Would that be fair? Absolutely not! Would the

Lord of all the earth do such a thing? I don't believe so. What good is the judgment at the end of time if everyone has already received their reward or punishment?

The wonderful message of the Bible is that both the good and bad are quietly "sleeping" in their graves until the resurrection day. At that time, they will be brought forth to face the Lord in the judgment.

> So man lies down and does not rise. Till the heavens are no more, they will not awake nor be roused from their sleep. Oh, that You would hide me in the grave, that You would conceal me until Your wrath is past, that You would appoint me a set time, and remember me! If a man dies, shall he live again? All the days of my hard service I will wait, till my change comes. You shall call, and I will answer You; You shall desire the work of Your hands (Job 14:12–15).

What About the Parable of the Rich Man and Lazarus?

Of course, astute Bible readers will point to Luke 16:19–31, where Jesus offers a fascinating picture of heaven and hell. Let's take a closer look at this parable…

There was a certain rich man who was clothed in purple and fine linen and fared sumptuously every day. But there was a certain beggar named Lazarus, full of sores, who was laid at his gate, desiring to be fed with the crumbs which fell from the rich man's table. Moreover the dogs came and licked his sores. So it was that the beggar died, and was carried by the angels to Abraham's bosom. The rich man also died and was buried. And being in torments in Hades, he lifted up his eyes and saw Abraham afar off, and Lazarus in his bosom. Then he cried and said, "Father Abraham, have mercy on me, and send Lazarus that he may dip the tip of his finger in water and cool my tongue; for I am tormented in this flame." But Abraham said, "Son, remember that in your lifetime you received your good things, and likewise Lazarus evil things; but now he is comforted and you are tormented. And besides all this, between us and you there is a great gulf fixed, so that those who want to pass from here to you cannot, nor can those from there pass to us." Then he said, "I beg you therefore, father, that you would send him to my father's house, for I have five brothers, that he may testify to them, lest they also come to this place of torment." Abraham said to him, "They have Moses and the prophets; let them hear them." And he said, "No, father Abraham; but if one goes to them from the dead, they will repent." But he said to him, "If they do not hear Moses and the prophets, neither will they be persuaded though one rise from the dead."

There has been much debate in the Christian world over the true meaning of the story of "the rich man and Lazarus," spoken by Jesus. The various arguments would be quickly resolved by settling a single issue: Is the story a true tale of the characters involved, or is it a parable?

Those who understand the story as literal argue that it demonstrates that life continues immediately after death, either in heaven or hell, before the return of Jesus Christ, and that hell is a place of eternal torment. Those who consider the story as a parable tend to look for the spiritual meaning rather than the literal one. Why is there such confusion?

For one, the story follows a long line of parables told by Jesus in the book of Luke. In chapter 14, we find the parable regarding prominent places at the dinner table, the parable of the great banquet, and several parables about the cost of following Christ. In chapter 15, we find the parable of the lost sheep, the parable of the lost coin, and the parable of the prodigal son. Chapter 16 includes the parable of the shrewd manager and then shares the story of the rich man and Lazarus. The story's position relative to the other parables implies, contextually, that it is also a parable. However, the others are specifically mentioned as parables, whereas the story of the rich man and Lazarus is not. This change in the Bible's language, despite its context with the other parables, causes some to believe that the story is to be understood literally.

So how do we determine which is correct? Let us first identify the things that must be true, according to the story, if it is literal:

- The righteous dead go to live in Abraham's bosom

- The wicked dead are able to speak despite their torment

- Those in hell can speak to those in heaven, and vice-versa

- The dead in heaven and hell both have bodies

- A drop of water is expected to relieve the torments of hell

Abraham, though faithful, was just a man like any other. In order for all the righteous dead to go live in his bosom, he would have to be quite large! The "fixed gulf" between heaven and hell is apparently not so fixed as to prevent communication between them, according to this story. And the flames of hell are apparently so weak that those in hell can carry on normal conversation and expect that just a drop of water would soothe them! That is hardly a picture of "torment." Finally, the Bible says plainly that the righteous dead will receive real bodies at Christ's return (1 Corinthians 15:51, 52), and the risen wicked a thousand years later (Revelation 20:5), so this story, taken literally, would contradict the plain words of the Bible by giving real bodies before the second coming. In light of all this, it seems clear that the story cannot be literal and, therefore, must be a parable.

Why would Jesus not plainly state that the story is a parable? First, let's identify His audience. According to verse 14, Christ is speaking to the Pharisees. The Pharisees believed and taught many things that were not according to the Scriptures. Among these teachings was that the Jews, upon their death, would go to Abraham's bosom to live in paradise. This variation of the belief in an immortal soul had its roots in the kingdom of Babylon, not in the Scriptures, and was not universally accepted by the Jewish people. (For example, the Sadducees, another leading religious group, disbelieved in any resurrection at all.) Therefore, because Christ was speaking specifically to the Pharisees, He used their own language to emphasize His point.

The Pharisees also viewed earthly wealth as a sign of God's favor. Thus, when Christ told the story about the rich man going to hell while the beggar found comfort in heaven, He was directly attacking this idea. In combination with the language of Abraham's bosom, the Pharisees knew exactly what Christ meant: The Pharisees were incorrect in their traditions, understandings, and teachings.

Christ repeatedly drew His listeners' attention back to the Old Testament Scriptures

(John 5:39; Matthew 22:29; Luke 24:27). Therefore, we should also look at the abundance of scriptural evidence that supports the sleep of death, awaiting the resurrection, to draw our conclusions about death, rather than a single story that is illogical unless understood as a parable. Most important, Christ Himself taught that the dead sleep in their graves until they hear His voice at the second coming (John 5:25).

It is clear, then, that the parable of the rich man and Lazarus does not support the idea of immediate life in heaven or hell after death. So what was Jesus teaching us in this parable?

The Pharisees are symbolized by the rich man feasting on the word. They had the Scriptures and a knowledge of the truth. But they had no concern for the Gentile nations, symbolized by Lazarus, who were around them starving for the crumbs of truth that fell from their table. Then, in an obvious twist of irony, the beggar dies and goes to Abraham's bosom symbolizing the Jewish place of reward. Conversely, the rich man dies and goes to Hades, the Gentile Greek place of torment.

The Pharisees thought they were saved by simply possessing the Scriptures, but they were not following God's command to love their neighbors. It's interesting to note that in the closing lines of the parable, Jesus says if they don't believe Moses and the prophets, then neither would they be persuaded though one should rise from the dead. Even though Jesus rose from the dead, the stubborn Pharisees still did not believe. It's also interesting to note Jesus did raise a man by the name of Lazarus and the religious leaders wanted to kill him to destroy the evidence of Christ's power (John 12:10).

The Appearance of Moses and Elijah

Did you know the New Testament shares that Peter, James, and John climbed a mountain with Jesus one day and had a major celebrity sighting? They saw the prophets Moses and Elijah talking with Jesus!

So you might now be asking, "If the dead do not go directly to heaven, then why did Moses and Elijah appear to Christ and the apostles on the mount of transfiguration?"

Did you also know the last prophecy in the Old Testament says, "Remember the Law of Moses, My servant. ... Behold, I will send you Elijah the prophet"? (Malachi 4:4, 5). Then in Matthew 17:3 and Mark 9:4, the Bible shares that these two individuals appeared to Jesus and some of the disciples.

So if the dead sleep until the resurrection, how did Moses, who the Bible says died thousands of years before, get to heaven? The answer can be found in Jude 1:9, where we read that Michael the Archangel actually resurrected Moses: "Michael the archangel, when contending with the devil he disputed about the body of Moses" (KJV). Plus, Jewish tradition says that three days after Moses died, the Lord came and resurrected him.

Of course, most Bible readers know that Elijah did not die at all, but went to heaven in a fiery chariot (2 Kings 2:11). So while most people are sleeping in their graves, there are a few notable exceptions. So who else is in heaven? We also know that Enoch was taken to heaven without dying because he "walked with God" (Genesis 22–24; Hebrews 11:5).

We also need to remember that there was a special resurrection after Jesus died on the cross. Matthew 27:52, 53, says, "The graves were opened; and many bodies of the saints who had fallen asleep were raised; and coming out of the graves after His resurrection, they went into the holy city and appeared to many." But that was not a universal resurrection—it was a special local resurrection for a very special purpose. The mass exodus from the grave is going to be when the Lord descends from heaven.

"Absent From the Body"?

In 2 Corinthians 5:8, the apostle Paul writes, "We are confident, yes, well pleased rather to be absent from the body and to be present with the Lord." This has been used by many to show that once the saved die, we go straight to heaven.

It's true that the language Paul uses here seems to imply that life after death exists apart from our bodies and will continue on in another form. To understand this passage, we must understand all that the Bible says about the nature of the human body and also about Paul.

We must be especially careful when using one or a handful of verses written by Paul to prove a point of doctrine, especially when the language used is ambiguous. The apostle Peter warns us in 2 Peter 3:15, 16,

> Our beloved brother Paul, according to the wisdom given to him, has written to you, as also in all his epistles, speaking in them of these things, in which are some things hard to understand, which untaught and unstable people twist to their own destruction, as they do also the rest of the Scriptures.

67

In other words, if we aren't careful, we might end up twisting Paul's writings to our own destruction. Instead, we must look deeply into this text to see what it truly says. When doing that, we see that the text in 2 Corinthians 5:8 does not actually imply that to be absent from the body means to be present with the Lord. One does not equal the other. Here is the entire passage in question, verses 1–8, so that we can understand the full context:

> For we know that if our earthly house, this tent, is destroyed, we have a building from God, a house not made with hands, eternal in the heavens. For in this we groan, earnestly desiring to be clothed with our habitation which is from heaven, if indeed, having been clothed, we shall not be found naked. For we who are in this tent groan, being burdened, not because we want to be unclothed, but further clothed, that mortality may be swallowed up by life. Now He who has prepared us for this very thing is God, who also has given us the Spirit as a guarantee. So we are always confident, knowing that while we are at home in the body we are absent from the Lord. For we walk by faith,

not by sight. We are confident, yes, well pleased rather to be absent from the body and to be present with the Lord.

Here Paul likens our mortal bodies with an "earthly tent" and says we should not worry if it is destroyed because we have a "building from God" that awaits us. This does not support the claim that we will be in God's presence without a body; rather, Paul simply says we will not have this body. He likens our bodies to clothing that we wear. In verse 4, Paul says he does not want to be unclothed (without a body), but rather further clothed (a different body). That's quite a different picture than a disembodied spirit that lives on after death!

When we compare this language to 1 Corinthians 15:51–54, also written by Paul, it becomes even clearer. The passage reads:

Behold, I tell you a mystery: We shall not all sleep, but we shall all be changed— in a moment, in the twinkling of an eye, at the last trumpet. For the trumpet will sound, and the dead will be raised incorruptible, and we shall be changed. For this corruptible must put on incorruption, and this mortal must put on immortality. So when this corruptible has put on incorruption, and this mortal has put on immortality, then shall be brought to pass the saying that is written: "Death is swallowed up in victory."

Here, as in his second letter to the Corinthians, Paul uses clothing imagery to describe our bodies. We currently wear a mortal body, but in God's presence at the resurrection we "must put on" an immortal one.

So Paul makes a true statement when he says he prefers to be "absent from the body" and … "present with the Lord." When we stand in God's presence, we will not be in the same body we have now. And the Bible tells us that this transformation will happen in a moment, in the twinkling of an eye, at the last trumpet. Although we all will die, we will sleep in death, and the next conscious thought we will have after death is when Jesus sounds the trumpet of God, when we are raised from the dead and when we will put on immortality.

So technically, as far as a saved person is concerned, their next conscious thought after death is the presence of the Lord. It will seem like three seconds to them. But as the Bible shares, it hasn't happened yet for those of us who live in this world's dimension of time because Jesus has not come yet.

When we consider all of Paul's writings as a whole representation of his beliefs, we see that his position on life after death perfectly supports the notion that the dead are asleep at death and await their bodily resurrection at the return of Jesus Christ.

The Coming Judgment

Consider how confusing it would be if rewards and punishments are already being applied to those who die. What purpose would be served by a resurrection? Obviously, each soul would already have a determined fate, and the final judgment spoken of by Christ and prophesied in the book of Revelation would be totally meaningless. Wouldn't it?

All the assurances heard at funerals about loved ones in heaven right now, while well-meaning, are simply repetitions of Satan's first lie to the human family. The portrayal of immaterial souls flying away from the body at death is not really a source of comfort to grieving relatives. Instead, in 1 Thessalonians 4:16, the apostle Paul describes the time when the righteous dead will be caught up to the Lord: "For the Lord himself shall descend from heaven with a shout, with the voice of the archangel, and with the trump of God: and the dead in Christ shall rise first." And he concludes by saying, "Comfort one another with these words" (verse 18).

Here is a perfect picture of true comfort, so we need to understand clearly what words Paul was referring to that would bring such comfort. "Then we who are alive and remain shall be caught up together with them in the clouds to meet the Lord in the air. And thus we shall always be with the Lord" (1 Thessalonians 4:17).

As Paul here describes, the coming of Jesus and the resurrection of the saved as being the manner and means of being with the Lord, he automatically excludes all other means of doing it. Then he admonishes us to "comfort one another with these words."

Indeed, would it be reassuring to believe that unsaved relatives are suffering the torment of unquenchable fire right now? Is there solace in the picture of loved ones looking down from heaven upon the heart-breaking circumstances of those left behind? No wonder Paul was so specific in describing the return of Jesus and the resurrection as the only way anyone can be with the Lord after death and, incidentally, as the only way to be comforted at their departure.

Paul's declaration points to the good news that death and the grave are not the end. There will be an awakening from the sleep of death. The righteous will receive the gift of immortality, but it will all happen "in a moment, in the twinkling of an eye, at the last trumpet. For the trumpet will sound, and the dead will be raised incorruptible, and we shall be changed. For this corruptible must put on incorruption, and this mortal must put on immortality" (1 Corinthians 15:52, 53). All the dead will rise to face the great judgment. Whether they went to sleep five thousand years or five minutes before Jesus appears, the wait will seem as only a fraction of a second for everyone.

Some have questioned the way in which Christ can restore the broken, decayed bodies of all the deceased through all the ages. Some were blown to bits in explosions, others were burned up in fires, and many went down into the depths of the sea. Will this present any problem for the mighty Creator of life to bring back every soul and restore each personality? None whatsoever. He who numbers the hairs of our head, counts the sparrows, and names the stars in the sky will have no difficulty in restoring the unique identity of every soul who has ever walked the earth. You can trust Him!

Why This Matters Now

The deception of counterfeit signs and wonders is one of the cornerstones of the devil's kingdom. He has worked powerful miracles down through the ages through people who claim to receive their power from the spirits of the dead. He's worked through the magicians of Egypt (Exodus 7:11), so-called sorcerers (Daniel 2:2), and through spiritists (Acts 16:16–18).

Revelation 18:23 clearly warns that in the last days, Satan will again use these manifestations, as he did in Daniel's day, to deceive the world. Claiming to have a message from heaven, demons will pose as loved ones who have died, saints, Bible prophets, or even the apostles or disciples of Christ (2 Corinthians 11:13) to deceive billions into rejecting God's clear Word— to follow false beliefs and manmade traditions, to believe that sin really isn't so bad. Those who believe the dead are really alive, in any form, will most assuredly be easy targets for this deception. After all, if the dead can give us messages straight from God in heaven, do we really need the Word of God to show us the light anymore?

Jesus said, "For false christs and false prophets will rise and show great signs and wonders to deceive, if possible, even the elect" (Matthew 24:24). These spirits of devils will work incredibly convincing miracles (Revelation 13:13, 14). The universal response will be to believe that Christ and His angels are leading out in a fantastic worldwide revival.

The only ones who will not be deceived are the ones who know the Bible truth (Acts 17:11). God's people will know from the Scriptures that the dead are really dead, not alive in any form. Spirits of the dead as ghosts do not exist. Therefore, God's people will reject all miracle workers and teachers who claim to receive special "light" or work miracles by communicating with these "spirits of the dead."

That's why it is vitally important that today you commit to believing the Bible truth so that you won't be deceived, so you will know that "if they speak not according to this word, it is because there is no light in them" (Isaiah 8:20 KJV).

Death, the Last Enemy

God is love. In the beginning, He made all things good. Indeed, God calls His creation of life very good! Death was never part of His plan ... death is an enemy.

That's why Jesus came, to not only save us from the penalty for sin, which is death, but also to purchase for us, with His perfect life and sacrifice, admission to a world where death and dying are no more.

Inasmuch then as the children have partaken of flesh and blood, He Himself likewise shared in the same, that through death He might destroy him who had the power of death, that is, the devil, and release those who through fear of death were all their lifetime subject to bondage (Hebrews 2:14, 15).

Everywhere Jesus went, He brought healing, life, and truth. And death is an enemy that will ultimately be executed:

The sea gave up the dead who were in it, and Death and Hades delivered up the dead who were in them. And they were judged, each one according to his works. Then Death and Hades were cast into the lake of fire. This is the second death (Revelation 20:13, 14).

The Bible says "the last enemy that will be destroyed is death" (1 Corinthians 15:26). Let's look forward to that day in truth!

FINAL MYSTERY

The Truth About Death Revealed!

Part Two

Heaven

Most people know the first five words of Genesis, "In the beginning God created ..." But few people know the last five words of Genesis: "... in a coffin in Egypt" (Genesis 50:26).

What God started as a paradise, because of sin, concluded in a coffin. Fortunately, the last two chapters in the Bible have much to say about a new paradise to come and the possibility of eternal life. Likewise, I don't want to conclude this book talking about death.

The monarch butterfly is known for its extraordinarily long migrations, which it makes twice in its two-year life span. During the summer, millions of monarchs can be found fluttering from Canada and the United States to their winter home in central Mexico—traveling in some cases more than 2,000 miles!

I believe that in many ways, God has also placed this inner yearning in you and me to migrate to a better place.

Throughout civilization, humans from all backgrounds have longed for a better world. Undeniably, nurturing visions of utopia appears to be a powerful, nearly instinctive desire within us. We are all in search of a better place, a world where there is unity and harmony.

You've probably sensed this desire in your own heart. Even during the best of times, we often find ourselves with some lingering feeling of discontent. In times of distress, these longings can become overwhelming. Think about when all your best efforts to improve your life seem stymied by forces or events out of your control, or when a loved one dies an untimely death.

Is it a wonder that so many desperate souls report visions of heaven? Perhaps it is simply to give us hope for a better world than this one.

Well, I do have good news: Heaven is for real.

God's Real Plan for Paradise

Heaven is all about returning the human race to our original home in Eden—but much,

much bigger and better! The Bible says, "For since the beginning of the world men have not heard nor perceived by the ear, nor has the eye seen any God besides You, who acts for the one who waits for Him" (Isaiah 64:4).

No human since Adam and Eve has ever seen the fullness of God's plan. He wanted the earth to be like Eden, and He gave three tremendous gifts to our first parents—a sinless life, a beautiful home, and dominion over the earth. They could have possessed those gifts forever by choosing to obey God, who intended to make the human family eternally happy.

But when sin befell the human race, those gifts were withdrawn. Adam and Eve began to die; their dominion passed into the hands of Satan; and they were driven out of their garden home. The first three chapters of the Bible present the picture of this great loss. The entrance of sin and the story of the fall of man is excruciatingly told in the first three chapters of Genesis.

Yet the good news is that the last three chapters of the Bible picture the exact opposite—the restoration of all things. The exit of sin and Satan and the removal of the curse is depicted in Revelation 20 to 22.

Snapshots of Heaven

Just before His death, Jesus comforted His disciples with this promise: "Let not your heart be troubled; you believe in God, believe also in Me. In My Father's house are many mansions; if it were not so, I would have told you. I go to prepare a place for you. And if I go and prepare a place for you, I will come again and receive you to Myself; that where I am, there you may be also" (John 14:1–3).

Don't these words bring comfort to your heart—that Jesus is, at this moment, preparing a beautiful home for you in a place where peace, love, harmony, and unity really exist?

The Biosphere 2 is a state-of-the-art greenhouse complex built on three acres in the Arizona desert. This huge, sealed, computer-controlled environment was intended to be a miniature version of the much larger Biosphere 1, which we call "Earth."

Completed in 1991 at a cost of $200 million, Biosphere 2 contains five wilderness areas ranging from a rain forest to a desert and stocked with thousands of exotic plants and animals; the eight human "biospherians" were to learn how to live off the land, isolated from the outside world except for communications. The designers envisioned Biosphere 2 as the first step toward human colonization of Mars through man creating the "perfect environment."

But when this landlocked Noah's Ark set sail for its two-year voyage of discovery, it ran aground on a host of unforeseen environmental and human disasters. Oxygen levels inside the complex dropped so low, emergency oxygen had to be pumped in, violating the main tenet of isolation. And crop production was so poor that the starving crew got hungry enough to steal food from one another or have it smuggled in. Nearly all the birds and animals that were supposed to thrive inside died—except for "crazy ants" and cockroaches that now fill the place.

The proud vision of man making up his own utopia on earth had become a joke. Today, Biosphere 2 is a tourist attraction masquerading as science.

History shows that mankind has been utterly unable to manufacture this kind of place. All of its best efforts have always ended in disappointment. All the greatest political, military, economic, and spiritual leaders have not ever come close to forging a true-to-life Shangri-La.

But God will be successful. "With men this is impossible; but with God all things are possible" (Matthew 19:26).

So now that we know it's just a matter of time, what exactly will this heavenly home be like? Many people picture heaven as a somewhat eerie place where ethereal spirits sit around on clouds, wearing halos, and strumming golden harps. I don't know about you, but frankly, this depiction sounds pretty boring to me!

Fortunately, the Bible gives us quite a different picture. Several passages in Scripture provide some fascinating insight into the heaven that's to come. You see, God wants us to know that heaven is a real place; and better yet, it's more real and more fulfilling than anything we've ever known or imagined.

The Bible speaks of a beautiful city called the New Jerusalem, which will be God's headquarters. It is described in Revelation 21 and 22. The picture these chapters paint is mind-boggling! First, the city is huge. It stands 375 miles on each side! (If placed on this earth, New Jerusalem would cover most of North Carolina, Virginia, West Virginia, and Maryland, and parts of Ohio, Pennsylvania, and Kentucky!)

Second, the city is incredibly beautiful. It has magnificent walls made of solid jasper. It has 12 foundations, each made from a different type of precious stone, including sapphire, emerald, topaz, and amethyst. And each of the city's 12 gates are made of a single giant pearl.

The streets of the city are made of a gold so pure that it appears as transparent glass. But we also learn that the streets are not made to simply look at and admire. Zechariah 8:5 says that "the streets of the city shall be full of boys and girls playing." Not only will New Jerusalem be a breathtaking, shimmering sight, it will also be a place to have fun and rejoice.

But most wonderful, God Himself will dwell among the redeemed within the midst of the city, and a glorious rainbow surrounds His majestic throne (Revelation 4:3). From beneath His throne, the river of life springs, and on both sides of this river, the tree of life produces a fresh crop of different fruit every month.

Activities of the Redeemed

It's also clear that you won't just be sitting around in the New Jerusalem, twiddling your thumbs without something to do.

They shall build houses, and inhabit them; and they shall plant vineyards, and eat the fruit of them. They shall not build, and another inhabit; they shall not plant, and another eat: for as the days of a tree are the days of my people, and mine elect shall long enjoy the work of their hands (Isaiah 65:21, 22 KJV).

An important aspect will be the biosphere of heaven: Its lifecycle will be eternal, not one cursed with the decay and death of this sin-infected world. The Creation story makes it clear that all of those negative biological processes entered our world as a result of sin (Genesis 3:17–19). Thorns will not be around in heaven to pierce your hands, nor will thistles scratch at your feet. Bugs will not bite, and leaves will not die. Sure, it's a little daunting to comprehend how all this will work scientifically–but our minds are limited by what they're familiar with. Heaven will change all that too. There are so many miraculous marvels in this world, it shouldn't be hard to believe that God can do what He is promising, including eliminating the effects of sin.

Indeed, our brains will certainly never get bored in heaven; there will be more to see and do than we ever imagined here on earth—enough to stimulate our minds for eternity. We'll be able to trace our family tree right back to Noah and Adam. We will be able to personally visit with many of the heroes of history we've only read about before (Matthew 8:11).

Furthermore, God and His angels will be there to answer many of the questions that have perplexed us here for millennia; we'll probably have questions we didn't even know there were to ask! We will also have an endless list of fascinating things to study. Perhaps Shakespeare said it best when he wrote: "There are more things in heaven and earth ... than are dreamt of in your philosophy."

Animals in Heaven?

One of the beautiful benefits of this utopian ecosystem will be that animals will not prey upon one another for food. We are told,

> The wolf also shall dwell with the lamb, and the leopard shall lie down with the kid; and the calf and the young lion and the fatling together; and a little child shall lead them. And the cow and the bear shall feed; their young ones shall lie down together: and the lion shall eat straw like the ox (Isaiah 11:6, 7 KJV).

And further,

> The wolf and the lamb shall feed to-
> gether, The lion shall eat straw like
> the ox, And dust shall be the serpent's
> food. They shall not hurt nor destroy in
> all My holy mountain," Says the LORD
> (Isaiah 65:25).

Obviously, there is no death among the animals either. This also quite literally means that
there will be pets in heaven. In fact, every animal could potentially be a pet because none
of them will be wild; they will not be afraid of
us, nor us of them. We have probably all had
to bid a sad farewell to some earthly pet. That
will never be a problem in heaven!

God does everything perfectly, and in heav-
en, everyone will find complete love and hap-
piness—including companionship with God's
other creatures.

People often wonder whether their pets
and furry friends from earth will be with them
in heaven. Some say this is impossible because
animals don't have immortal souls, much less
souls. But as we've learned, that's just not true.
So if the all-powerful God of the universe
wants to surprise and delight us with the gift
of resurrected kittens, puppies, horses, fish,

rabbits, birds, snakes, turtles, or whatever other critters we love on this earth, He is certainly able to do so! By granting this, in no way would He violate His moral absolutes. We'll just have to wait and see.

Celebrating with Friends

Human exploration of the cosmos and space travel will know no limits. The book of Hebrews declares that Jesus created all the worlds seen and unseen (1:2). Astronomers estimate there are about 100 thousand million stars in our Milky Way galaxy alone. Outside that, there are millions upon millions of other galaxies also with billions of stars each! So it would seem plausible that we will find other inhabited worlds, and visit with other intelligent created beings! Isaiah also says of our world: "He created it not in vain, He formed it to be inhabited" (verse 45). Those other solar systems must be "created not in vain" as well. They light a multitude of worlds.

Another scriptural clue about life on other planets is found in Job 1:6. "There was a day when the sons of God came to present themselves before the LORD, and Satan came also among them." In Luke 3:38, Adam is called "the son of God." It's quite possible that the "sons of God" in that heavenly council are the first created beings from other planets. Adam should have represented earth, but Satan usurped his birthright. Fortunately, Jesus, the second Adam, redeemed what was lost by the first Adam to Satan (1 Corinthians 15:46). We cannot state positively that this is what the passage in Job refers to, but many in the Christian world agree this scenario is possible.

The Bible also assures us that the righteous loved ones we lost here on earth will be raised to join the living in God's kingdom (Isaiah 26:19; 1 Corinthians 15:51–55; 1 Thessalonians 4:13–18). Being reunited with loved ones is undoubtedly one of the things we will enjoy the most. Imagine just how deeply moved you will be when a baby or child you lost will be brought to you and placed in your arms! And think about looking into the eyes of a parent, spouse, or close friend who has passed away and then embracing their vibrant, glorified bodies and knowing you will never need to part again.

Heavenly Music

Thrilling music is often mentioned in connection with heaven, so you can be sure that playing instruments and singing God's praises will be a big part of our eternal experience. Our Creator is one capable of immense diversity; all creation testifies to this truth. I'm sure we'll enjoy an endless variety of delightful music, and we won't just be limited to playing harps!

The Bible even says that God Himself will sing: "The LORD your God in your midst. … He will rejoice over you with gladness, He will quiet you with His love, He will rejoice over you with singing" (Zephaniah 3:17). He also gives many instructions for us to sing, such as in Psalm 100:2: "Come before His presence with singing." It would make sense then that the angels who also worship Him would come before Him with singing too. It's going to be a wonderful concert to hear in heaven!

Marriage and Children in Heaven

Some find it disconcerting when Jesus says there will be no new marriages in heaven (Matthew 22:30). We shouldn't deny, cover up, or worry over this concept; He ought to know since heaven is His hometown.

First, let's be careful not to assume this passage means that God will hand divorce papers to the redeemed who have had harmonious marriages as they first enter the pearly gates. Knowing who God is, that He is the very essence of love, whatever type of relationships we have now will be even more intimate and fulfilling in heaven than anything we have experienced here. I think we can trust in Him to plan something wonderful that will not disappoint us.

There also might not be any new births, but we know from the Scriptures that there at least initially will be children in heaven. Isaiah describes heaven and mentions children several times (11:6–9). Malachi 4:2 says that we shall "grow up as calves of the stall." This seems to indicate that the resurrected children of heaven will experience a physical maturing process going on as well as a spiritual one. Of course, we shouldn't forget that no matter how "old" we get in heaven, we will always be eternally young and full of vitality. We will never suffer the terrible effects of aging that we must endure on this corrupted earth!

Face to Face with God

Of course, the ultimate and culminating experience of heaven will be meeting our Creator God face to face. "Then shall I know even as

also I am known" (1 Corinthians 13:12 KJV).
Revelation 21:3, 4, explains:

> I heard a great voice out of heaven say-
> ing, Behold, the tabernacle of God is
> with men, and he will dwell with them,
> and they shall be his people, and God
> himself shall be with them, and be their
> God. And God shall wipe away all tears
> from their eyes; and there shall be no
> more death, neither sorrow, nor cry-
> ing, neither shall there be any more
> pain: for the former things are passed
> away (KJV).

This is the God who created our world
and us in His image. He mourned when mankind fell, and He's also the one who rescued
us through Jesus. His unsurpassed love moved
Him to implement a powerful plan: to enter
into our world, suffer the results of our sin,
and then to die for us. And now, as He makes
preparations for us to go home, He longs to
shine the way and fulfill all of our hopes.

That's why, in many ways, a perfect world
would be pure misery for anyone whose heart
was not converted—who didn't learn on earth
to love what God loves. If you don't turn away
from the things that cause Him grief now, what

makes you think you will want to please Him in heaven? Ultimately, God always honors our choices; He's not a tyrant as some believe.

As for now, God's chosen people waited 4,000 years for the Savior to come the first time. That seemed like a terribly long time, and many lost hope. But He did come. It's a historical fact. And if He came the first time, according to His promise, we have no reason to doubt that He will come again just as He says He will. He will always do what He promises. You can count on it.

Heaven Begins Now

Until that day, rejoice knowing that we don't have to wait to experience all the benefits we'll have in heaven. "Peace on earth, good will toward men" is not just a "pie in the sky" that the angels sang about. Knowing what lies ahead, that our future is secure in God's hands, we can have a powerful sense of joy and peace right here and now. Even though we won't see peace among the nations on this earth, we can still have peace in our hearts amidst the chaos.

For those who make contact with God in a personal way today, heaven begins now. As Jesus said, "The kingdom of God is within you" (Luke 17:21). He also said, "He who hears My word and believes in Him who sent Me has everlasting life, and shall not come into judgment, but has passed from death into life" (John 5:24).

God is the Friend who never forsakes us; the Counselor with all the answers; the Partner in all our endeavors. He cleanses us from sin, and when we ask, He imparts the power we need to transform our selfish lives into lives of love. That's the kind of heaven we can live in right now.

God is good; He is our heavenly Father who wants eternal life and the very best for His children. Unfortunately, death is an enemy that came into our world (Romans 6:23). Yet the Lord is desperate and willing to save us if we would only trust in Him and cooperate with His plan.

"For God so loved the world that He gave His only begotten Son, that whoever believes in Him should not perish but have everlasting life" (John 3:16). There you have it. Two choices: everlasting life or eternal death.

When you die or Jesus comes, whichever happens first, your next conscious thought will be rising in one of two resurrections—the resurrection of life, when the dead in Christ rise, or the resurrection of condemnation, for the unrepentant and rebellious.

Because God so loved you, He gave His only Son to save you. Now your eternal destiny depends upon what you choose to do with your temporary gift of life that you have right now.

Please, why don't you ask the Lord today for that gift of life that will never end?

"Yea, though I walk through the valley of the shadow of death, I will fear no evil; For You are with me." —Psalm 23:4

Are the dead really dead?
Discover the truth
about heaven, hell,
death, the afterlife, and
out-of-body experiences at
www.isheavenforreal.com.